THE LOGAN NOTEBOOKS

The Mountain West Poetry Series
Stephanie G'Schwind & Donald Revell, series editors

We Are Starved, by Joshua Kryah
The City She Was, by Carmen Giménez Smith
Upper Level Disturbances, by Kevin Goodan
The Two Standards, by Heather Winterer
Blue Heron, by Elizabeth Robinson
Hungry Moon, by Henrietta Goodman
The Logan Notebooks, by Rebecca Lindenberg

THE LOGAN NOTEBOOKS

— POEMS —

Rebecca Lindenberg

The Center for Literary Publishing
Colorado State University

For information about permission to reproduce
selections from this book, write to
Permissions
The Center for Literary Publishing
9105 Campus Delivery
Colorado State University
Fort Collins, Colorado 80523-9105.

Printed in the United States of America.

Library of Congress Cataloging-in-Publication Data

Lindenberg, Rebecca.
[Poems. Selections]
The Logan Notebooks : Poems / Rebecca Lindenberg.
pages cm -- (Mountain West poetry series; 7)
ISBN 978-1-885635-37-2 (paperback) -- ISBN 978-1-885635-38-9 (electronic)
I. Title.
PS3612.I532743A2 2014
811'.6--dc23

2014011479

The paper used in this book meets the minimum requirements of
the American National Standard for Information Sciences-Permanence of Paper
for Printed Library Materials, ANSI Z39.48-1984.

1 2 3 4 5   18 17 16 15 14

Publication of this book was made possible by a grant from the National Endowment for the Arts.

ART WORKS.
arts.gov

for my Utah students,
with gratitude and affection

CONTENTS

THE LOGAN NOTEBOOKS

CLOUDS

Cloud shaped book, opening. Cloud shaped like a sphinx. Cloud shaped like a steam engine blowing steam. Cloud shaped like a UFO. Cloud shaped like a handbag. Cloud shaped like the first thing you spoke when we met. Cloud shaped like a peacock, or a cloud-breathing dragon. Cloud shaped like an old-fashioned clock. Cloud shaped like a rabbit chasing a crow. Cactus-shaped cloud. Lampshade-shaped cloud. Cloud shaped like your laugh. Cloud shaped like a roast chicken with wee chef's hats on its feet. Cloud shaped like a cartoon drawing of a cloud. Cloud shaped like a horse ridden by a monkey wearing oven mitts. Cloud shaped like Texas, or Wales. Cloud shaped like a comet. Cloud shaped like a fading demand. Cloud shaped like a boot, or a bottle, or a branding iron with a sun in the middle. Cloud shaped like a map of the sky. Cloud shaped like a rhapsody. Like a fever dream. Cloud shaped like a man helping a woman brush off her skirt, or a woman lifting her skirt, or a dance in which they become clouds.

IMPROVISATION (ARRIVAL)

He watches while I talk
about being in love

with the world—we sit
on concrete steps, leading down

to the door-well, a mess
of leaf-litter and tiny carcasses

of winged ants. I don't say
how I long to throw myself

into the deep groove
of the present,

like a needle in a moving record
and pick up the note of this life—

A neighbor's car idles, resonating
in our storm door. The clatter

of wings as two
dragonflies uncouple

the long exclamation marks
of their bodies,

I might not have noticed
if I hadn't seen it

reflected in his steel
blue eyes—their questioning

movements now follow
my hands. I gesture towards

this or this, meaning
just what I say and more.

SEPTEMBER

My guy stands beside a sign on our storm door, "No smoking within 20 feet. Oxygen tank in use,"
ashing into an empty brown bottle. A young trucker lives across the cul-de-sac with his pretty girlfriend.
She has a limp, and lends me her hairdryer. When he's home, he drinks until he's numb to his thunderous
sound-system, or shows us all of his guns. He coats his knives in anticoagulant. But one night he brought
out a high-power telescope and honey whiskey. We could almost see the popped bubbles in the moon's
concrete surface. His girl doesn't come out much when he's gone. He says she has an Internet addiction.
Then he tips a little of the honey whiskey back into him and says something about bedding Mexican
women while he was on leave in the Marines. Only he does not say "bedding" or "Mexican" or "women."

DIFFERENT WAYS OF SPEAKING

In Rome, *buongiorno* bends its knee and flourishes, a little *ciao* is a chirp of friendship. But I kept hearing this word, *salve* from hipsters, Communists. *Hail, citizen.* I remember the first time someone *salve*-d me from under his sunglasses. I felt so cool.

When my parents say *roof*, it sounds like *rough*. As in, the *rough* is leaking. Or, get down off that *rough* right now for God's sake those wings will never work.

Soda. Pop. Waterskimmer. Jesusbug. Cart, trolley. Stroller, buggy, pram. Pacifier or soother or binky or dody or babycork. Standing *on* line, as an imaginary thing drawn there, or *in* line, as bowling pins.

I offer to *babysit* our niece. My guy, to *tend* her. I like his version better.

From the other room, I hear the *abideeabideeabidee* of cartoon scurrying, and Yosemite Sam whistles *Jumpin' Jehosaphat!* When a few hours later a student cries out—*O my heck!*—I think of this.

Where I come from, a garment is a dress. Where I come from, a temple is where Jews gather on Sabbath. Or where Buddhists light incense and turn intricately carved prayer wheels. *Om mani padme hum.*

Our neighbor across the cul-de-sac says something about gays in the military. Only he does not say "gays."

Our neighbor says something about alcoholism in the Native American community. Only he does not say "alcoholism" or "Native American."

In "Politics and the English Language," George Orwell says, "If thought corrupts language, language can also corrupt thought."

Salve, ragazzi. Salve, nemici. Om mani padme hum.

Robin comes home from school one day, panting, "Okay, so. I say *yellow* and you say *yellow*. But what if what I actually see when I say *yellow* is what you see when you say *blue*? And we can never actually know." And I remember the same question blowing my mind. Still does, it's just, now I've read some Wittgenstein.

IMPROVISATION (DISTORTIONS)

Distortion, or, error. To err is to wander.
      —Lyn Hejinian, "A Thought Is the Bride of What Thinking"

Today, my voice tuned to a new
channel in a language I barely speak,

said things I don't think.
This one book claims the author

is dead. But I don't want to be
dead, I want my naked foot to feel heat

in the dirt of this grass-bald yard.
I want to sit without fidgeting

in the wild silence of grief, to notice
the crow, silver-black as bark char,

eyeing long grasses where
ducklings just hatched, and

how white wine in the bottom of this glass
is the same temperature as the glass

when it's empty. I want a *you*
for one reason to attend to these

details that might later
divert you. My gaze goes to the black

bee, big as a hummingbird
purring at my umbrella's hem—

a dot without its question mark.
Do you want to be my you?

It's not hard. Poetry is nobody's
native language. Or the only one.

APHORISM

Sometimes the best way out of the rain is into the river.

THINGS FOUND IN A LOCAL GROCERY STORE

Seasoning for homemade elk or antelope jerky. A friend explains this is a gimmick. You just need salt, sugar, maybe some garlic powder. She adds as an afterthought, *It's really low-fat.*

Muhammara, a paste of red pepper, pomegranate molasses, walnuts, olive oil, cumin. Simmer with chicken, or scoop with bread. A handsome young Lebanese man hand makes it. It's the same rust-red as the Southern Arches and, like them, suggests sun.

Next to the freezer aisle, with its soy burgers and supreme pizzas and crinkle-cut fries, there's a food storage aisle—rows of coffee cans, all babyroom pastel, labeled Dehydrated Taco Meat Substitute, or Chocolate Beverage Powder, or Eggs. A tagboard promotional sign reads Church Bulk Orders Available. When the zombies are picking their teeth with the rest of the world's finger bones, Utah will be safe in its basements, feasting on reconstituted mashed potatoes.

There's the usual stuff—pink tomatoes, bagged salad darkening in the corners, pale gelatinous salmon or flaccid little gray shrimp, cemented butter, batteries, packets of dried hollandaise or onion soup mix. Jars of fancy pickled cauliflower with tiny hot red pepper flakes suspended in the oddly viscous juices. Nail polish remover. Mouthwash.

And there's a deli counter, cold glass guarding a bowl of Frog-Eye Salad, wobbly mix of tapioca and little mandarin orange crescents. There's a ham studded with maraschinos and pineapple rings, a lasagna that seems to have cottage cheese in it, and two salads garnished liberally with fake bacon. *What bomb shelter did they haul this out of?* My sister wants to know.

But there's one little wooden trellis shelved with loaves of bread whose flaxen crusts you could knock like a door, bejeweled with purple olives, or cloves of roasted garlic soft as cheese, or else confettied with an anthology of seeds. They are as warm and heavy as genuine optimism.

We buy a couple of bison ribeyes, a garlicky pillar of local goat's cheese, beets, butter lettuce, a Virgin of Guadalupe candle. Behind the checkout, one of my students greets me with his Bugs Bunny grin, *What's up, Doc?*

LETTER TO A FRIEND, UNSENT

I haven't written   in a while
because I don't want to talk
                about anything
I've been unable to stop
thinking about: the knotted thread
        of bad capillaries on my retinae,
money, or that my morning was ruined
by the unusual tightness
        of jeans around my thighs,
                        like the obligations
of having a body
so ill-fitting, oppressively snug
        around an obstinate will.
And while   I don't want
        to be distracted
from this Duchamp thing
I've been working on—   I am
itched out of reverie
                over and again
        by this feeling I don't deserve
my raptures anymore.
So I'm sorry. I don't want to
        bring you down. It's unfair
to have to hear about needles
and envelopes and flies
        when you might just have been
enjoying an iced tea outside
        and when I would prefer to tell you,
                really,

there's a family of pheasant living
         in the massive cottonwood
we call the Tree of Life.
The male's red, green, gold plumage
                  makes him look
      like a Christmas present
I would want to give you.
So except "I hope you're well,"
                              that's all.

BEAUTIFUL THINGS

I came to talk you into physical splendor
I do not wish to speak to your machine
　　　　　—C. D. Wright, "Key Episodes from an Earthly Life"

The evening we spend trying—replaying the Internet video—to learn the steps to "Thriller." Barefoot on a linoleum floor under a naked bulb, between a deep exhausted laugh and a swig of purple wine from a box, I realize I don't feel alone.

When, after plucking fine weeds from the tomato patch all morning, I reach up to scratch my cheek and my skin still smells like sunned-on vines.

Gramophones are beautiful. Anatomical models of the heart are beautiful.

The canyon, in summer. With my sister and her husband, we sit by the river eating bread and cheese and drinking apple-juice-colored beer. The sun's doing its thing with leaves. We're all a little red-handed from tree-climbing, my guy keeps throwing his knife into the dirt. It sticks some of the time.

Many stones are beautiful. Obsidian, grooved like an old record. Agate, like a cross-section of water. Candy-banded malachite.

Scrimshaw is beautiful. Horrible and beautiful.

A walk on a winter beach, snow along the water's edge trimmed with a thin filigree of seaweed, like so much unraveled cassette tape. Salt-stain across the toe of a boot. The coin-cold tang of raw oysters drizzled in vinegar.

We were in this field, where wild spring onions grew. Everywhere we stepped, we crushed pale shoots into frost-softened ground and the air tingled with their faint savory smell.

Old glass soda syphons are beautiful. Olivewood spoons are beautiful.

If a woman with an exquisite face has a bad amateur haircut, somehow it makes her all the more beautiful.

The Salt Flats make vast mirages that seem to flood the road. You can see the mountain range, the clouds reflected in them. They seem so whole.

Little silver fillets of *boquerones*, pickled with garlic and parsley, olive-oiled and forked onto torn bread. Small *almejas*, baby clams steamed with bacon and green wine—we pluck their pink tongues. Things you can only find in the places where they come from, rare and impossible to replicate here, are beautiful and haunt me.

The Tree of Life in our backyard is beautiful because it holds up a swing. No, because it conceals the pheasants. No, because it drops its leaves in the creek. No, because you love it. No, because everyone loves it. No, because its origins are a mystery. No, because it is ours. No, it is not beautiful? O, it is beautiful. It is beautiful.

Arguments may be elegant, but exclamations are beautiful. Sometimes these include language like *Hosanna!* or *Goal!* Sometimes it is someone closing his eyes.

TREES

The slender umbrella pine holds its florets high over our heads. I stab lamb smoking on the grill while Craig and Robin set seed cones ablaze, hurl them down the bocce court into the purpling dusk. *Is that wise?* I raise my voice. *I really doubt it*, Craig hollers—grinning—back.

Spine-limbed Joshua Tree, did you know you're a lily? Yes, you could say I'm on a vision quest.

Those trees in the front yard of my California childhood dropped spiky little seed pods that looked like the club-end of a mace, or like tiny blowfish. Mom called them "sputniks." *O, O, satellite of love.* Sometimes the tall grass concealed them; we'd step on one barefoot and howl.

Coming back from Zion through the Grand Escalante, we drive into the high forest, mostly Ponderosa and Fir but as we round a bend we find a massive stand of Quaking Aspen, their chartreuse leaves flickering. You make me feel that way, you know.

We'd put our feet on the rail of the white balcony, push back onto the hind legs of our green plastic chairs, sip white wine from nice glasses. And that massive cottonwood sheltered us from sun, from view of those on the street below. Come fall, the great black tree would start to fritter away its leaves, but then Don would come and sit and say, *God bless this home. God bless this tree.*

IMPOSSIBLE THINGS

It is impossible to be comprehensive.

THINGS FOUND IN *THE PILLOW BOOK OF SEI SHŌNAGON*

A poem that someone has composed for a special occasion or written to another person in reply is widely praised and copied by people in their notebooks. Though this is something that has never yet happened to me, I can imagine how pleasing it must be.
      —The Pillow Book of Sei Shōnagon

An ox driver who hates his oxen. Last year's paper fan. Birds.

The Melia and the wild pear. Duck eggs. A large tree that has been blown down in a gale and lies on its side with its roots in the air.

The face of a child drawn on a melon. Coughing.

Embarrassing Things. Surprising and Distressing Things. Things That Lose by Being Painted. Clouds.

A High Court Noble's carriage with its dirty blinds. The way in which carpenters eat. A woman who wears sleeves of unequal length. A certain lieutenant. People of bad reputation, though you have to keep your guard up. *Such people often give a more sincere impression than those of good repute.* Priests. The voice of someone who blows his nose while he is speaking. The expression of a woman plucking her eyebrows. Her Majesty, the Empress. His Excellency, the Chancellor. Common people. Wet nurses. A friend.

The Ministers of the Left and of the Right.

One has gone to bed and is about to doze off when a mosquito appears, announcing himself in a reedy voice. One can actually feel the wind made by his wings and, slight though it is, one finds it hateful in the extreme.

A heron, *with a most disagreeable expression in its eyes. Yet, though it has nothing to recommend it, I am pleased to think it does not nest alone in the Yurugi Wood.* The red-headed sparrow, the kinglet. The mandarin drake, sweeping the frost from its wings.

Love and hate, as things that cannot be compared. But you can feel them for the same person— sometimes at the same time. Then again, maybe that's why they cannot be compared.

On one occasion a man, who invariably sent me a letter after we had spent the night together, declared he saw no point in our relationship and had nothing more to say to me. When dawn appeared without the usual next-morning letter, I could not help feeling rather gloomy. Then in the evening, a child arrived with an open umbrella in one hand and a letter in the other. I opened the letter and read with more than usual haste. "The rain that swells the water" was the message, and I found this more charming than if he had sent me a whole sheaf of poems.

Winds and Wind Instruments. Shrines. The Festival of Young Herbs. The Festival of the Blue Horses. The Chrysanthemum Festival and the Iris Festival and the Hollyhock Festival. And the Weaver Festival, wherein everyone writes poems for the Weaver and the Herdsman. Held on the one clear evening each year when the Weaver may cross a bridge of magpie wings to join her beloved, just for one night, on the opposite side of the Milky Way.

An allusion, in a spray of rained-on pear blossoms, to *The Song of Everlasting Regret*.

Things That Are Distant Though Near, like *the last day of the Twelfth month and the first day of the First.* Also, Things That Are Near Though Distant, like *Paradise*.

"Why so silent?" said Her Majesty, "Say something. It is sad when you do not speak."
"I am gazing into the autumn moon," I replied.

"Ah, yes," she remarked. "That is just what you should have said."

18

IMPROVISATION (NOSTALGIA)

Even in Kyoto—
hearing the cuckoo's cry—
I long for Kyoto.

       —Matsuo Basho, trans. Jane Hirshfield

Afternoon breaks
like a fever.

Cool air billows—
a dark sheet

snapped open,
ripples heat wears
into it all day

shaken out. Not blue

that has a name

but like a Moorish dome
painted to resemble it, inlaid

with legions of stars

and the moon.

A plate of rice
for which I'll hunger.

DÍA DE LOS MUERTOS

This apartment is like a comic book version of a shitty apartment. It's dark, the wood paneling is tickered with nail holes, the tiles in the bathroom loose as teeth. One fell through yesterday. Through to what, you ask? The gutter between comic book scenes? The space between thought and mentioned? Don't ask. I buy sun-colored flowers and set them around. The next-door neighbors leave their three-legged dog chained to a pickup most of the time. Two women live there. One is missing an arm but goes to work in scrubs. The man who lives there wears a cowboy hat and cowboy boots and high-waisted jeans and I have come to understand that chaining the animal to a truck might seem to him a reasonable compromise. There aren't a lot of handbag-sized dogs around here, but more than your average number of folks who've wrung the neck of their own chicken. My guy comes home, he says, *I got the bread and coffee—man, Sally's such a bitch. Something smells good, what is that?* He reaches down to scratch the candy skull tattooed on the back of his calf. I say, *Chicken?*

IMPROVISATION (AWAY)

The world is full of lost places—
you know you're there

when nobody can find you,
not even the dead.

The valley is a rich furrow

terraced with crops, orchards
farmers read from left to right
under savaging sun.

Flies whine
in the streets, in the hours

when the water is off. At night,
dark blue and beheavened

with stars, a black cat
stalks long-necked geckos

across uneven orange roofs.

There is no Eden I'd prefer to these

long days so much away, steep
white streets blank as any page

I've never written.

ON A VISIT TO ROBERT SMITHSON'S SPIRAL JETTY

All the new thinking is about loss.
In this it resembles all the old thinking.
             —Robert Hass, "Meditation at Lagunitas"

We pass the Golden Spike monument, joining this and that America and my guy says, *I can't believe I'm gonna be a man who wears jewelry.*

I find myself thinking about regret. But I find myself talking about pie.

A passing pickup kicks a stone into the wheel-well of the Subaru, which screeches like a wounded creature. We pull over, he checks something, checks something else. A minute later, the car kicks the stone back out.

When we get to the parking lot, our penny-colored pit bull trundles out of the backseat, and the three of us pick a way over rock-rubble to the lakeshore.

Today, a coral-tinged froth gathers like snowpack on the Great Salt Lake's ragged sandline. No, not like snowpack, exactly. More like cappuccino foam. The dog samples a mouthful, then shakes herself.

The jetty curves into the viscous lake, dark rocks gathering towards the horizon—diminishing train of a far-off gown.

Air coming over wet sand tastes like an old tin can.

The sky is a bright, stark white and in the wind, the first pinch of winter.

And while we stand there, that wind picks up and lifts heaps of pinkish foam into the air, blasts them apart like a beautiful explosion, except everything is so quiet we can hear the dog's jaws click as she rears up to catch some of that ineffable fluff.

I find myself talking about pie again. I find myself thinking: *Blackberry. Blackberry.*

APHORISM

Getting to know someone is like wearing a headlamp—you won't see what you don't shine on.

THINGS THAT LOSE BY BEING WRITTEN ABOUT

Snow escaping our footsteps. Snow melting out from under itself. Clockworks, though they are very beautiful and tempting to write about. Halcyon days.

Pulling out a sweater that still smells of last winter's perfume. The sound of a slow-moving river. Being a woman, which is fairly easy as long as no one's around.

The slight smell of jasmine tea on a very cold morning. The sound of a cat jumping from a high window. The sound of someone taking a guitar out of its case.

A strange desire to touch embers in the fire pit. They wax orange when you blow on them, like recognizing something as true.

Lyric, which is a kind of defiant logic and moves like a crowd. The crack of ice melting in a glass of rye. The strident scent of conifer. Any idea of home.

THINGS THAT GAIN BY BEING WRITTEN ABOUT

Abstractions, such as happiness or identity. Unexpected things. How those relate to happiness and identity.

Clouds and billboards and other things that change.

Plants whose names do not do them justice, such as Bindweed or Dill. Definitions that become more accurate in their expansion.

Feasts, just for the pleasure of it. Longing, because writing can lessen it. Different kinds of goodbye.

BILLBOARDS

Outside of Amarillo, a chalk outline on a black sign advertises a company you can call to clean up dead bodies after an accident or a suicide or crime. I think, Texas. I think, Who does this job in places that aren't Texas? I remember General Sheridan said, *If I owned Hell and Texas, I'd rent out Texas and live in Hell.*

Along I-15 in northern Utah, billboards for: Laser hair removal. Breast augmentation. Chemical peel facials. Cosmetic dentistry. Liposuction. Foolproof weight-loss supplements. Planet Fitness. Old Country Buffet. Human growth hormone treatments. Doctor John's Adult Boutique. Online education, GO TO CLASS IN YOUR PAJAMAS. Which my students do, anyway. Including the ones with breast augmentation.

Hauling a trailer across Missouri, we pass under a massive cross. My father says, *Holy shit. That must be the buckle of the Bible belt.* Near there, a billboard reads: GOD'S PLAN FOR MARRIAGE = I MAN + I WOMAN FOR LIFE. I think, How romantic. We also see: SIGNS OF OVARIAN CANCER. ABORTION STOPS A BEATING HEART. CENTRAL MISSOURI STOP HUMAN TRAFFICKING COALITION. GENTLEMAN'S CLUB NEXT EXIT. PASSIONS EROTIC COUPLES STORE. And: JOIN THE PURITY PLEDGE.

Not a billboard, exactly. But up and down the narrow roads of South Dakota, from the Badlands to Sioux Falls, little black and white triangles read, THINK. This marks where some drunk flipped his Trans Am, or where the sleepy driver of a pickup veered into an oncoming station wagon, or where some kids in Mom's minivan distracted each other into a ditch. But everybody was okay. Because where everybody was not okay, where the cops had to cut through metal to get the body of a local cafe owner out of her Chevy, or where the guy just out of prison and his girlfriend were crushed into the dash of her Toyota, the little white and black signs read, WHY DIE? Which, when seriously confronted, I don't think works as a rhetorical question.

From Evanston and with increasing frequency towards Laramie, Wyoming: Little America. Little America. Cheap gas. 50 cent cones. Lots of room. Little America.

CLOUDS

Cloud reflected in a rearview mirror. Cloud reflected in the screen of a cell phone that gets no service on these roads. Cloud reflected in a window that reads: *For sale: Goats. For milk or meat.* Cloud reflected in a window that reads: *2-for-1 Breakfast All Day.* Cloud reflected in a window that reads: *Guns! Guns! Guns!* Cloud reflected in a window that doesn't say anything, and in a broken window. Cloud reflected in your mirrored sunglasses. Cloud reflected in a watch-face. Cloud reflected in still water pooled in a gas station parking lot. Cloud reflected in the mirror I use to apply my lipstick. Cloud reflected on the black lens of a camera. Cloud moving in the water of a black river. Cloud moving up the pebble-nicked windshield. Cloud we look past. What else is there to do.

THANKSGIVING

My guy buys brie, a baguette, and cherry tomatoes with his food stamps. I buy firewood and wine. We go up the canyon and light a fire in a stone fire pit and sit in soft folding chairs and talk for hours, let the penny-colored pit bull walk against the river current. And as we sit, the tall granite walls of the canyon slowly purple to black, and the sky goes out, and the flames we're sitting by get brighter and warmer, until we begin to dwindle, and we douse them, and we go.

THE HOUSELESS WOODS

November's black trees
fringe a less-black sky.

Snow blooms beneath
a whole moon.

I look for the fox
with a mangy tail—

No fox.
Just more light
than you'd expect.

Shoeprints
perforate the snow-field,

notation
for a wordless refrain.

Something tells me
the world will end
and everything

will be fine. Something
tells me these marks

were mine.

BIRDS

My sister bought her husband a "Show Chickens of the World" calendar from the dollar bin at Barnes & Noble. Now he calls her his Frizzle, after a bird whose baroque explosion of blond feathers somewhat resembles my sister's morning hair.

Crow sits on a curb, watches for a car to crack the nut it left there. He's a clever devil, with shiny black snaps for eyes.

We hear words in birdcalls. The American Goldfinch says, "Potato chip!" and the Ovenbird pleads, "Teacher! Teacher!" and the Ash-Throated Flycatcher croons, "Tea for two." The Eastern Meadowlark bids, "See you! See you!" Which just goes to show how words can take an expression of the soul and make it common.

I try to write about a cartoon Roadrunner. But an anvil falls on the page and leaves a giant and precisely anvil-shaped hole where the words were supposed to go.

BIRDS AND MEMORIES OF BIRDS

After brunch of omelets with salsa and coffee flecked with cinnamon, we take Robin to the aviary. It's a little sad, the off-pink flamingoes fed just enough shrimp to keep them blush, the cooped eagle with its seraphic wingspan. Shrill little budgies. But peacocks roam free, unfolding themselves to us. One was pure ivory. And a lone duck looks confusedly from his awkward vantage atop another bird's cage and Craig ventriloquizes, *Um, guys? A little help here?*

On the outskirts of Rome, a murmur of starlings seethes in defensive patterns, choreographed around falcons planted to thin their population. They school and swerve and behave like wind.

It was one of Craig's memories from childhood in Okinawa, along with his bigwheel and the caterpillars that left welts where they slid across the skin. Along with the scorpion fish hovering near the diving platform, and the monsoon shutters. The cockatoo in his cage croaking, *Hi, Charlie! Hi, Charlie!*

Walking towards the church in Murano, we pause to watch a pigeon walk through a puddle, poop, then turn and drink from the water it just bobbed through. My sister looks at me and says, *You know you're a pigeon when.*

IMPROVISATION (PRAYER)

people
be
come
un

      —E. E. Cummings

Night confines
me to room, thought
to me, bird to nest.

Every year
I forget how to leave
a little, little more.

I remember
lying in an open-
windowed chamber

listening to you
whistle back
at dawn-stirrings

in the trees. O
how I wish
what I can't stop

wishing for. Or to stop
wishing that, but still
be able to wish—

a way to open
whatever room
let stale night

air out. I thank
all the taloned gods
it doesn't matter

what I wish. In the end
birdlight always
breaks through.

MOUNTAINS

Like cracking a whip the size of a conveyor belt. Then its echo, the sound of all the bookcases in all the world bumping back against their walls. No. Like the god of noise stamping his hoof in a marble hall. Or, imagine the winter sky is the tight skin of a drum, thumped by the gunshot. The penny-colored dog looks up, looks at me, goes back to eating snow. My coffee, even through the paper cup and the cup-shaped paper around it, is hot. I sip while the sound pulls itself apart in the trees. Then another, knocking all over the granite canyon. I know it's just some kids too close to the road, firing a shotgun at bottles or rocks. But it's still the sound of a heavy-haunched creature being put down. Or it's the sound of a great rural indignation. Or of some dread teenager's heart backfiring. Or a hundred schoolchildren turning to see what clicked open the door.

ON SAFETY

In the trunk of the car, we keep: A hatchet, two sleeping bags, a gallon of water, matches, gas can, tampons, bungee cord, headlamp, jumper cables, winch, wrench, glucose, windex, a pack towel, a first aid kit with Cipro and burn ointment, an empty paint can because who knows, salt for snow, salt for food, Sriracha sauce, frost-scrapers, umbrellas, toilet paper, goggles, three kinds of tape, an old mason jar, a few books, and some rubber gloves. So far, the only thing we haven't used is the gas can.

If you do make ghost pepper salsa again, remember: It'll take a day to pant it out.

Now and then, you'll find yourself at a party with some stoned end-time thinker pretty sure he has a foolproof plan for surviving the zombie apocalypse. One time, a snowboarder with big shoulders was all, *No offense, but like, you're diabetic. Survival of the fittest, man.*

I wanted to but did not say: Darwinian fitness has nothing to do with how much you can bench-press, but rather the traits most likely to help a whole species survive. Like curiosity, innovation, social cooperation, even affection.

Also: Your hair looks kind of stupid.

Instead, I said: In that case, I might as well have another Manhattan.

THE WEST

I'm sitting on my bed, a Victorian ruffle of pink and yellow, reading *To Kill a Mockingbird* and I hear it. Like a big rig barreling into the neighborhood. I stand to look out the window, and the street comes rolling like a picnic blanket shaken towards me. Then the ground bucks under me, I grab the bedframe, make my way under a desk like we'd drilled in school. And then it's over. There's a tsunami in the toilet, and a fissure through the carport floor. We go outside. Our neighbors come out and sit on the lawn—one, an EMT, has her radio, so we learn—the mudfill under the Marina district jellied in the tremors, its mansions sliding into the sea. Part of the Bay Bridge opened like a trapdoor. Candlestick Park, packed with fans raising foam fingers for their two home teams, cracked. People poured forth into the field. And a two-kilometer stretch of the Cypress overpass, cakelayers of highway jammed with traffic, smashed down onto itself. That was the first time I felt the strange elation of utter rupture, when something happens that is so scary, it is too much to feel. You sort of float around like a cartoon thought-bubble over your own head, watching other people try to fill theirs with something. Anything, really.

APHORISM

There may be ruined fences, but there are no ruined stones.

POETIC SUBJECTS

The capital city. Arrowroot. Water-bur. Colts. Hail. Bamboo grass. The round-leaved violet. Club moss. Water oats. Flat river-boats. The mandarin duck.
          —*The Pillow Book of Sei Shōnagon*

The sky. And the sky above that. The exchange of ice between mouths. Other people's poems.

My friend says we never write about anything we can get to the bottom of. For him, this is a place arbored with locust trees. For me, it's a language for which I haven't quite found the language yet.

The dewy smell of a new-cut pear. Bacon chowder flecked with thyme. Roasted duck skin ashine with plum jam. Scorpion peppers.

Clothes on a line. A smell of rain battering the rosemary bush. The Book Cliffs. Most forms of banditry. Weathered barns. *Dr. Peebles. The Woman's Tonic,* it says on the side, in old white paint.

The clink of someone putting away dishes in another room.

The mechanical bull at the cowboy bar in West Salt Lake. The girls ride it wearing just bikinis and cowboy hats. I lean over to my friend and say, *I would worry about catching something.* And he leans back to say, *That's really the thing you'd worry about?* We knock the bottoms of our bottles together.

How they talk in old movies, like, *Now, listen here. Just because you can swing a bat doesn't mean you can play ball.* Or, *I'll be your hot cross if you'll be my bun.* Well, anyway, you know what I mean.

Somewhere between the sayable and the unsayable, poetry runs. Antidote to the river of forgetting.

Like a rosary hung from a certain rearview mirror. Like the infinite rasp of gravel under the wheel of a departing car.

Gerard Manley Hopkins's last words were *I'm so happy, I'm so happy.* Oscar Wilde took one look at the crackling wallpaper in his Paris flat, then at his friends gathered around and said, *One or the other of us has got to go.* Wittgenstein said simply, *Tell all my friends, I've had a wonderful life.*

THE WEST

We read about daredevil priests, conquistadors in finned helmets and shin guards, fur traders selling otter pelts to railroad barons, Chinese laborers, gun-slinging good-natured whores. We rooted for abalone beads in old Indian midden heaps. We tidepooled, toeing anemone to watch them pucker. On Gold Rush Day, in bonnets and petticoats, boots and cowboy hats, with pie-tin props we panned for gold in sand-bagged baby pools, traded fake treasure for a bowl of PTA chili at the cardboard-front Saloon. On one family trip, a darkly tattooed man in a wife-beater forbade my sister and me to go anywhere near the open mineshaft. Mom heard dueling banjoes whenever he spoke, but we liked his soup. We hiked the High Sierras, learned to stanch a wound. We learned to swim out of riptides, how to pop a dislocated elbow back, vinegar a jellyfish sting, or better, not get stung in the first place, snapping like bubble wrap the air sacks in kelp washed ashore. We did the Pledge of Allegiance in English and Spanish. We did the Lord's Prayer in English and Spanish. Jenny Chin and I ate our after-school wontons with ketchup. It wasn't all bonfires and guitars, of course. In fifth grade, a girl from sixth grade was killed on the train tracks; in sixth grade, a jogger was mauled to death by a mountain lion. And I got the diagnosis I've still got, if worse now. But I also got my first kiss off a Mormon kid in front of Bob's Donuts. I'm thinking about these things in the car, rocketing across the same Nevada wasteland where, at thirteen, my father taught me to drive. It's studded with brothels and un-blown-up bomb-testing sites. My guy says, *Yeah, but. You didn't grow up in the Real West.*

THE REAL WEST

The frontier is productive of individualism. . . . The tendency is anti-social. It produces antipathy to control, and particularly to any direct control. The tax-gatherer is viewed as a representative of oppression.
      —Frederick Jackson Turner

The guy who sells smoked trout at the farmer's market—he's got a Ph.D. in Classics, but he left his professorship for fish farming. *I was always interested in history,* he smiles, and his white beard bristles. *But never politics. This is more my speed.*

Cowboys and oil rigs. Knowing how to dig a firebreak. Or mill your flour. Or prep seed potatoes for planting. Or pickle beans. Knowing where to take the antelope you shot for butchering.

Rows of flat-slatted snow fence all along the I-80 corridor. Still, a blown-out big rig tipped into the ditch.

Yucca. Aloe. Ladies' night at the shooting range. Sage.

Sitting in steam rising off the hot springs, snow mounted all around, sipping wine while an eagle hovers above the river watching for a glint of fish.

I walk out of the university auditorium in Billings after the reading and drum circle, head back to the hotel with its bucking-Bronco carpet. The air is acridly sweet. *What is that?* I ask. *O,* says my host. *It's the sugarbeet factory.*

Mutton-buster kids at the rodeo, their little aluminum spurs.

Mobile-home meth labs.

Rows and rows of Big Jim chiles transubstantiating sun into heat. Buy them at a roadside stand, roast them over an open flame. They'll go into chile verde, tortilla soup, pizza, quiche, bagels, apple pie. And it'll all have that tangy savor, a little sting in the cheek, the sun inside warming your throat.

A church without a cross on it. A church with a cross and a statue of Our Lady. Our Lady of the Desert Passage. Our Lady of the Wildfire. Our Lady of the Snakeoil Salesman. Our Lady, Pride of the Penitent. Our Lady of the Snows. Our Lady of the Unknown Variable. Our Lady of the Birdsong. Our Lady of the Beggar's Ball. Our Lady of the Green Glass Sea. A church with a basketball court. A church in a warehouse, sign written in Korean. A church in a shopfront. La Iglesia Evangelica. La Iglesia Pentecostal. A double-wide church on a compound comprising bomb shelters and gunracks and bathtubs planted with tomatoes and mint.

A church whose plastic movie-times marquee reads: Get Right or Get Left.

A McDonald's with a smoking section. A church-run charity shop stocked with musty sofas, an armchair with some hard substance caked onto its wing, remoteless TVs, bins of bent shoes, bins of tinny kitchen equipment, beveled yellow water glasses, twee teacups.

A sign on the road that says: Bureau of Land Management. That says: Trespassers Will Be Shot. That says: Next Services 78 Miles.

At the coffee shop, a little clutch of hipsters wear their colored tattoos and ear gauges and expensive denim like they'd thought them up. A work-booted dude in a flannel shirt with his sleeves rolled up orders a chai soy latte. You notice his raw knuckles.

A taco cart in a Sears parking lot. A dim sum cart by the bus station.

In a dry arroyo miles from anything but lizards and scrub, a pair of beat-up Adidas. No laces.

A redrock spire. A redrock cliff, windowed with an arch. A butte like a stone ship run aground. Goblin Valley. Virgin River Gorge. Dead Horse Point. Moki Dugway. A canyon pass, at whose entrance a brass memorial plaque says: This Is The Place.

IMPROVISATION (BOY)

You thought you knew him.
        All those hackled black quills,

      tail feathers
that are eyes
blinking in their palms—

all that thunderous hooving

      didn't seem dangerous.

You thought
      you saw a wild-eyed he-child

with a birdcall
in the back of his chest
      and a rattle-work shield

      standing
over a fire, shaking
      No! I can do it myself!

at some implacable god.

But gods. Boys. Who
        can't know you back.

ON A VISIT TO NANCY HOLT'S SUN TUNNELS

There's not so much as sagebrush to squat behind. Just pale ground reaching through colorless air to a far uneven horizon. And these four huge concrete tubes.

We crack a couple of beers. Tailgating the winter solstice.

It's cold, though not yet the dark, soul-winnowing cold that it will be. I find myself thinking about extremes. But I find myself saying, *Is it really more important for you* not *to sit for a family photo than it is for your mother to have one?*

Every time I have to advocate for something I don't care about, it diminishes me.

I feel myself pulling in, away from the edge of my skin. I move closer to the fire.

You'd be amazed how much wood you burn. You'd be amazed how little wood you can carry. We're already starting to worry.

Our water is whitening to ice in its plastic bottles. My glucometer announces it is out of temperature range. But I want to watch sunrise align itself through two of these cylinders.

Later that night, I fall asleep in a tent too big for our bodies to warm, inside a sleeping bag, under a down comforter and a wool poncho, wearing all of my clothes. I'm woken just before dawn when ice crystals formed by my own breath melt down the back of my neck.

We stand in a gathering crowd as the sun slowly lifts its head through these giant sights. Cameras shoot and shoot. People stamp the ground and pant into their mittens. They sound like cold ponies.

Worth the pain in your hand-joints you can only feel in this kind of cold.

Somebody asks, *Is there enough fuel for a morning fire?* Somebody else says, *There's always something to burn.* It almost sounds true.

IMPROVISATION (GIRL)

I think she wanted to explain
                          the silence
          hidden
within her voice—

blue egg in the nettles.

          She wrote something

on a rock, used the rock
                    to bash in the skull
          of an injured deer.

Bloodied swan-neck arms.
                              She
slinks into her own viscera,

a baby fox
          backing into its trunkhole.

The wordbone's connected to the
          gutbone.

Meanwhile, her desire

          for nobody now
bucks like a rabbit
                    under her ground.

THINGS THAT DO NOT MATTER

The logo on someone else's T-shirt. Toenail polish or not. Irony. Which vodka. The relative positions of knives and spoons on a set table. How long it takes someone to move forward after the light turns green. How anybody takes their coffee. Having or not having heard of a band. Five or ten bucks either way. Whether the waitress is a little slow today, and any number of other things, which—if we can't bring ourselves to ignore them—become little quotidian obstacles to the sublime.

THINGS THAT MATTER

Physics. Whether or not you can see. Salt. The sublime. By what means people suffer themselves to be governed. The extinction of primrose or milkvetch or desert tortoise or lynx. Phosphorous. Promises. Insulin. Trying to know what matters and what doesn't matter. How you love.

TEMPLES IN THE WILDERNESS

I'm not allowed in the Mormon Temple but I'm told it isn't like the churches I'm used to—long, vaulted naves, choir screens and side-chapels. Instead, it's a manor of many different rooms, each to its ritual purpose—sealing a wife to her husband for eternity, baptism of the dead in a font upheld by a circle of stone oxen.

The interior of the Assembly Hall is all pine—what the pioneers had to work with. But the pillars are reverently painted to resemble veined marble, the pews, oak grain.

And thou shalt overlay the boards with gold.

If you drop a pin at the front of the Tabernacle, you can hear it fall from the last row.

We see this on our tour of Temple Square. A young bride in her Disney-Princess dress raises a newly bejeweled hand to her cheek for a photo, amid gardens almost funereal in their neatness. A doe-eyed sister missionary asks Jessica if she'd like to discuss her relationship with Jesus Christ. Jess blinks. Then says, *Well, for starters, we're both Jews.*

The synagogue in Rome is the only square dome in a city of cupolas. The first Jews came to Rome before the diaspora, esteemed dignitaries to Julius Caesar from the Kingdom of Judea. But then their descendants, walled off in the Ghetto, weren't granted citizenship until 1870. Kosher cheese in Rome isn't actually kosher. Or it's more kosher, since—unchanged—it predates the current rules.

I learned this from a woman who lived in the Ghetto. She also told me that when Nazis first arrived, they demanded payment. People in Rome contributed their gold—wedding rings, coins, watch chains, brooches, candlesticks, napkin holders, knives. For every donation, however meager, the rabbis wrote a receipt. Melted down, it came to just over the ransom. Not that it mattered.

And thou shalt overlay the boards with gold.

The Inca built the walls of their Sun Temple from massive black blocks, so precisely cut they required no mortar, slightly angled against the slope of the Andes. Earthquake after earthquake, European construction atop these blocks came catastrophically undone. But the wide-shouldered Incan foundations still lean into the clouds.

The bell tower of Kaiser Wilhelm Church remains a charred husk near the Berlin Zoo. Bombs killed all but a handful of the animals, starving Germans scavanged what they could.

He shall bring all things to your remembrance.

Aphrodite, Cytherea, Kypria. I have been to your temple, what's left of it anyway. There are poppies. Red poppies.

Come to me now. Loose me from hard care and all my heart longs to accomplish, accomplish. You. Be my ally.

APHORISM

A doctrine's a divining rod; a conscience, an echocardiogram.

A DECEMBER WEDDING

The ceremony begins before noon, the bride in a slinky gown and white cowboy boots, the groom in his Marine dress blues. On his side, everyone wears shimmery winter dresses, suits and ties and flasks. The Mormon side wears khakis, Christmas sweaters, long denim skirts. The bride's uncle says something about God's Plan for Happiness. I think, Not much of a plan. Then women with long braids bring out two tureens of soup, rolls, and cold cuts. On the way up to the groom's family home for some celebration later, my guy, loosening his tie and lighting a cigarette, says, *Well. They spared every expense.* But the young couple stood together in the snow for their photos like nobody else was there.

THINGS THAT LOSE BY BEING PHOTOGRAPHED

One night, when the moon is very full and sugaring the snow all over our backyard, there we are—a bearded man, and a small woman in blue rubber boots, dancing slowly to no music, while a penny-colored pit bull picks up first one foot, then the other, trying to tell us to let her inside.

THINGS THAT HAVE LOST THEIR POWER

Anyone who feels they have to lie. An adult asleep in their candy-colored childhood bedroom. A talented cellist at a karaoke club.

Someone who loves to read, but can't always see.

A penny-colored pit bull, carried from the car in the arms of her person—he could be so gentle. Her shaved leg with its black gash of stitches was still numb from knee surgery. She never whimpered, but she peed from the pain of it.

EARLY IN THE NEW YEAR

Today, according to the radio, the air quality in Logan will be the worst in the nation.

We go to dinner at a friend's house, overlooking the valley. You can see, from there, how it holds smog like squalid water in a clogged sink.

Gesturing with her glass of champagne, Irina tells us how she climbed into the backseat of her mother-in-law's car with a friend after Spanish class one day in Quito—letting her mother-in-law chauffeur them angrily home. *How was I supposed to know?* She laughs. *What does a young girl from Soviet Russia know about car etiquette? Like we rode in cars!*

On the way home, someone is rolling a massive tractor down the passing lane. Someone else idles for awhile in a parking lot. At a four-way stop, a monster pickup revs its engine.

I think, Clogged sink. I think, Like we rode in cars.

ON BEING COLD

Plenty of things can make you annoyed—being cut off by a truck whose bumper sticker reads, KEEP HONKING, I'M RELOADING. Grapes with seeds in them.

But anger is different. Frost crystalling the veins. Not a movement of the soul, but the soul failing to move you—to empathy, or at least patience.

While the soul hibernates, the rest of the body does weird things with itself. It mixes warm milk and brandy. Or it wears socks that look like gloves. Or it gets irrationally furious when the young man at the gym can't find your membership. Neither this young man with his thick hands nor even the girl on your usual treadmill has done anything wrong. You're just cold.

APHORISM

A little pain saves the hand from the flame, too much makes his hand the man's enemy.

MARCH MADNESS

A stranger in trouble is a gift from God.
                    —Arabic proverb

My students hand in their Spring Break papers. One kid who rides the rodeo circuit writes about inhumane treatment of animals—I keep threatening to turn him into a meme. One student writes an essay about her father, in jail for the molestation of his grandson. Another student describes guilt about his sister, raped by a classmate he thought was a friend. A young woman adopted by an upstanding Mormon family explains how her father murdered her mother. The police deemed the daughters, high-pitched as Greek priestesses, hysterical with grief, so wouldn't hear their testimony. An email was ruled unreliable, the father's affair, irrelevant. Another student writes the story of running away from home, where he was only welcome if he went to church. And one student writes about his exile from home, where too many young men upset the polygamy ratio. I take a break from grading to go to the grocery store, where I hear a woman with videogame hair say, *I could never live in a city. That's no place to raise kids.*

PLEASING THINGS

The unexpected kindness of a stern neighbor. Homemade bread. The first day of the year when you wake up—the same hour at which you always wake—to sun.

IMPROVISATION (THIS LAND IS YOUR LAND)

for Philemon Tevis

Phil is like, *No. There are some things*
black people just don't do—

camping is one of them. Not a lot
of sailing, either. Or line-dancing.

And why do you want to sleep on the ground,
no toilets anywhere? I'm like,

It's nice to get away from people?
Said the ax-murderer, Phil laughs.

We are sitting on my porch
eating chips and salsa, drinking beer.

A coyote hunting a housecat hides
behind a car parked on the corner.

Our conversation turns towards
the 3D printer Phil just used at the U,

how we've both heard you can
get one of those to print a gun.

Then to a friend, arrested for smoking
pot at home. He's a giant kid,

Navajo, and we're both worried
they'll throw the book at him.

I have some books I'd like to throw
back—*Civil Disobedience,* maybe,

or something not yet finished, wherein
Minute Men see their final hour, legislators

obsessed with virginity find
a purer calling in their stewardship

of Earth, money-hoarders will stop
blaming those they starve for being hungry.

And everyone and I will have nothing to fear
from any wilderness, but wilderness.

APHORISM

Sometimes you're the spaceship, and sometimes you're the barnacle.

OTHER WESTS

From the window of our plane over the Andes, it looks like we're always taking off or landing. We're way above the cloud-cover. But then, so are these black peaks. I watch a sheet of snow slide down one crag in great hunks, plunging out of view.

Driving out of Cusco into the Sacred Valley, Margaret and Luis and I pass the Municipal Stadium. Faded images of sportsmen spiking volleyballs, returning tennis serves, or leaning to one side to breathe as they lap across a pool encircle the crumbling compound. Luis cracks a joke, something about the Municipal Stadium keeping everyone's sense of irony in good shape.

Popcorn, a pisco sour. *Politically*, says the woman I'm talking with, *I am west of center.* Me too.

In Hawaii, raspberries have no thorns, poisonous spiders no venom. Flora and fauna that stowed away from elsewhere, here lose defenses they no longer need. It's very hopeful.

The Inca didn't have an underworld. They had a *mundo interior*, an interior world, transited by the serpent of wisdom. Death, its own West, makes us hungry for wisdom. And its opposites.

I suppose there's always Space. It's not west or east of anything. It's just away, outer. The only place still Other to us all.

Someday, I would like to get close enough to a pole that I can watch my compass needle twirl itself around, a ceramic ballerina in an old music box. Twinkle, twinkle, little star.

THINGS THAT ARE HARD TO DESCRIBE

I wake in late winter dawn, open my eyes to find there's something there. This has happened before, the black smudge and speckle of a hemorrhage in the vitreous. It blooms slowly across my view. Ink-leak into oil. How do I explain this so he'll understand? Bats flap in my face when I try. I know what's in store—the needle slides into the open eye, then the suddenly underwater look of everything when the drug goes in. I worry that someday a curtain of retina will tear itself down across the apron of my sight and leave me alone backstage. I could get all wrapped in the folds of that panic. So I drive slowly to the store for noodles and ricotta—his family is coming to dinner. When I get back, I drink a glass of wine, like putting little mittens on all the nerve endings. His family arrive, very sweetly ask how I am. As convincingly as I can, I lie.

ONE WEEK IN APRIL

A colleague's wife gets a ticket for swearing on the bus. The law specifies: Women. She is asked to disembark.

My guy says, *Loganistan.*

I give a reading at a university—it opens with a prayer. A nervous young man offers, *Dear Heavenly Father. Please help us to understand Rebecca Lindenberg's poetry.* I too ask for understanding.

At lunch later, a student explains that men here must have special permission to grow facial hair—say, a doctor's note explaining you erupt in welts if you shave. Then you're given a "beard card" to carry.

I think but do not say something that would get me a ticket on the bus.

WINDS

Voice snare. Hair churn. Wind under the soles of the feet. Wind that knows the names of all its loosed feathers. Nearly-wind in the wolf's fur. Tender wind handling the edge of a sleeve. Wind making instruments of these forgotten bottles. This rickety window. Tarp-snap. Hat thief. Dawn wind with ice on her skin. Wind that undoes ideas, like inside-outing an umbrella. Nap-snatcher. Breath-eater. Night wind in spring, with his outside hands. Candle-thief. Briefest of ghosts. Wind that carries your name, now. Wind that always carries your name. Wind with its hand on my back. Wind that simmers in the grass. That breaks around stars. Water-shifter. Bird-lifter. *Not I, but the wind that blows through me.* Reed-sounder, setting all those winged seeds free.

LATE MAY

You can plant after Mother's Day. Otherwise, the frost will take everything, as it did the sage that was trying to reimagine itself in my little herb trough. Now, it's just a stopped thought about twigs.

But the tarragon. It's a slender-leafed menace.

ON NATURAL HISTORY

On a long wall in the Utah Natural History Museum, fourteen enormous skulls stare down. This one wears an arched bone mitre, this one, a speared crown. That plated helmet is ridged with thorns. So many Ceratopsian dragons in the Great Hall of an invisible king.

On the way to Dinosaur National Monument in the family minivan, my father slows to a crawl. *What the,* he says, leaning forward over the steering wheel. A flickering black river of something swarms across the road. We all groan at the sound like crackling foil coming from under the wheels. At the next gas station, Dad asks the attendant if he knows what that was. *Sure,* he says. *Mormon Crickets. Some seasons, they come so thick you gotta put chains on your tires.* Mom says, *That's rich.* The attendant grins, *They're cannibals.*

Tyrannosaurus. Utahceratops. Excalibosaurus. Troodon. Stygimoloch, horned demon from the river of Hades. Argentinosaurus. Quetzalcoatlus. Archaeopteryx, the ur-bird, its miraculous feathers.

My sister and I poise in front of upheaved layers of Jurassic sediment; it looks like a gigantic cross-section of Neopolitan ice cream. Morrison Formation. Where the fossils mostly are. An approaching ranger says, *Hey. What do you think you're doing?*

My sister sends me a cartoon. One T-Rex uses his little T-Rex arms to say to a fellow T.-Rex, *I love you* this *much.* And that other T-Rex says, *That's not very much.*

In the Utah Museum of Natural History, there's a giant slab of yellow stone under thick glass—you can stand on it, look down at the weird reptilian patterning in earth-preserved skin. I find myself thinking about monsters. But I find myself talking about psychology. He is a cartoon T-Rex. I am a cartoon tumbleweed. Seriously. What do I think I'm doing.

MORE PLEASING THINGS

A little cat asleep on your lap while you read Foucault in a big orange chair.

Cutting back the wild mint. Cutting back the lavender.

Coming home from long travels to find your guy waiting for you with a new bottle of whiskey and an evening's worth of porch-stories—a friend who got caught cheating, again. A funny thing that someone said about her son. Some dumb dog-and-cat antics. How he missed you.

WINDS

It starts with a moth lifting off. Or a child clapping, or a woman shaking a rug. Brickfielder. Chinook, a kind of Foehn. Boreas and Argestes. Harmattan. Mistral. Nor'easter. Papagayo. Sirocco. El Niño. Williwaw. Zephyrus. And after the debris is piled away, sand swept from the stoop, porch furniture righted, ships patched and again sea-worthy, it settles. A single petal coming undone, a woman holds a cold drink to her face. I wade alone through long grass in a still, still dawn.

There's an old Impala, and a *Ghostbusters* station wagon. There's a car that looks like it's right out of the pages of the *Great Gatsby*—it even has wooden wheelspokes. Naturally, there is a jeep fully equipped with machine gun and cannon. But there's also a little vintage teardrop trailer, hitched to a Volkswagen Bug. There's a shop selling expensive ladies' clothes, but I too want to look like I'm on the set of *Grease*, so I peruse. As I do, an announcer calls them, *Clothes from when ladies looked like ladies and didn't just give it all away.* On the way home from the classic car show, we get stuck in traffic behind all the Studebakers and El Caminos and Model-As pulling away, but I get a chance to admire the chrome angel ornament on the front of a Rolls-Royce before it occurs to me, itching, that I could canoe faster than this. At a party in one of the fancy mansions on Center Street, the owner of the Rolls, dressed all in white, describes that as his "around town" car. *So,* I say, knocking back a mint julep. *I take it you're not from around here.*

INSECTS

That summer, all the dogs had pearlescent mustard guts in the corners of their mouths. As the cicadas' electric purr died, their husks plopped softly to the ground, sidewalks aglitter with shattered fragments of thorax and wing.

Dawn had been researching bedbugs. She explained they don't only hide in beds, but even mobile phones and computers. (As I write this, I eye the tiny seam between keyboard and key.) Xhenet says, *When I lived in New York, my roommate's boyfriend had bedbugs. She came home one day and said, "Oh, man, I have this really itchy mosquito bite." And I was like, "Oh God. Just set yourself on fire."*

Bronze soil. A line of black ants, each flagged with an emerald green trapezoid of leaf. I dismount my horse to crouch alongside the tottering single-file line. *Leaf-cutter ants,* says the vaquero. He follows the queue to this rustled mound, big as a new grave. *There,* he says, pointing.

It's early and thinking only of coffee and Ezra Pound, I go down to the car with keys in my hand. On the seam above the driver's side door, a night-stiff praying mantis. I move it to the garden, wipe dew-damp from my hand on the side of my jeans.

In his library, he had framed glass cases holding many species, pinned to white paper in order of size. Beetles, spiders, butterflies and moths, scorpions and crickets and bees. Splayed, labeled. He called that "his collection." I guess this is mine.

APHORISM

Why swat at the bee already whirring for a window?

TREES

Dust, sun, scrub oak—my childhood smells. We hike among fluted pillars of huge Sequoia. The Grizzly Giant, the Bachelor and the Three Graces. Because of the way fire shaped its legs, the Clothespin Tree. My guy and I pause to have a photo taken by the Faithful Couple. But in a hot tub later that night, his voice full of someone else's words, he tells me he's been unhappy. He says, sipping a cocktail I just got him, that he resents me. I have been unhappy, but I didn't blame him. I guess he didn't blame him either. I should be angry that he's telling me here, but I still have on my skin the smell of those infinite trees, some of whom I've known my whole life. They soften me. The Fallen Monarch. The Galen Clark Tree. The California Tunnel with a road cut through—its roof still weeps, like an infected wound. The Telescope Tree. Like old gods, proper and indifferent and perhaps if I sing the right chords, one of them will turn me into wood now.

IMPROVISATION (DEPARTURE)

We talked across the early dark, cold air
finally some relief from the heat

we'd been trying to unstick ourselves from.
We raised what was left

of our night-flavored talk and drank—
I put the tip of my tongue against an ice cube,

held it to the bottom of the glass.
Then we got in the car. He'd said,

I want this place to speak its name to me.
I'd said, *I just want the walls to stop falling.*

Our words hung there in the air
like the smell of rain after a skyfit.

On the radio, a windy-voiced man panted
over the sound of his guitar.

We were quiet while the car
windows framed first houses, then houses

in various stages of unbuilt, then
storage units and call centers, ramshackle

barns and midden heaps of rusty implements,
then wide fields brightened by their sprinklers

arching over them in a kind of silent pageantry,
here and there a huddle of cows in a mudpatch.

The coffee at the diner was so weak it shone red
in the sun when the waitress poured it.

The only other folk sat at the counter
in dirty work boots, ordered specials,

while he and I, opposite each other
in an orange booth, reached out with forks

to take a bit of this or that biscuit, sludgy
with white gravy, or egg-yolked steak, offered

in place of any more hard-belled syllables.
We agreed, we both hunger

for that heightened state that requires
your attention on any given morning—

to sun, the smell of warm buttermilk,
an ache in the spleen portending sorrow,

to a tiredness that should only belong
to youth or certain other emergencies,

to the thin, hot coffee, the not-quite-said-yet
good-byes that will ache like snakebite.

THE END OF AUGUST

To avoid getting ink stains on the notebook into which one is copying stories, poems, or the like. If it is a very fine notebook, one takes the greatest care not to make a blot; yet somehow one never seems to succeed.
        —*The Pillow Book of Sei Shōnagon*

A friend looks me over critically. He says, *Nobody who makes this much of a mess could be anything but sincere.*

I say, *I hate sincerity.* And I mean it.

MOUNTAINS

Sara and I trundle along the trail, passing back and forth a question about how happiness might be related to leniency. I've been on this trail in many seasons. After his wife—his favorite model—died, Monet stopped painting people. He stood before the Rouen Cathedral in morning drizzle, or as the sun downed behind no cloud, and watched it vary. His shadows never render black but a yellower shade of white, or stone-mauve, a kind of thunderous gray. He said, *Color pursues me like a constant worry.* In January these mountains make a winterous cathedral, revealing how many kinds of bright there can be. Right now, they are timorous green getting ready to fan out fall's gypsy textile flicker of magenta, vermillion, chartreuse, gold, and the barks of trees will blacken with damp. *You'll find someone else,* Sara says. But all I want is to see the same landscape a thousand times and never repeat myself. To know the difference between white and white.

MOUNTAINS

Star-white. Nymph-white. White as the jawbone of a deer, at least I think it was a deer, I found near here. White as not-knowing. Lightbulb-white. Spit-white. White as a vow. Powder-white. White as a high C. White as one of grandma's ceramic figurines. Whale-white. White as a martyr's foot. White as a babytooth. White as a claw. Picket-fence-white. White as a hot coin. As a fear. White as a blind eye. Soap-white. Wildflower-white. White as the inside of an eggshell. Mime-white. White as a washed wall. Fat-white. Ash-white. White as a description of silence. White as a new hate. Label-white. White as broken ice. White as a glint off a silver dish. Ghost-white. White as riverchurn. As the dashed line down a highway along the river, those two black tracks through snow as white as forgetting I was ever here.

APHORISM

Just because you can aim doesn't mean you should spit.

THINGS YOU CAN NEVER HAVE BACK

That tall man with a little red birthmark under his eye. I remember I loved watching him drive his Volkswagen through snowstorms, small muscles of wrist and knee and clavicle taut at attention, but his conversation so calm and calming. That person he brought out in me.

Money I squandered on whatever, I can't remember now. Rent, coffee, the good eggs. Glasses for somebody else. A couple of paperbacks. Shoes. Anyway, it's gone.

Spent.

The edges of my retinas, lasered away in hopes of saving the rest of my vision.

A certain kind of panic—that nerve, like the high string on a violin played a little too long, snapped.

The trailer is too full. He keeps saying, *It's just fucking stuff. Leave it, or throw it away.* Two decades' worth of red journals kept since high school, into the bin. Three big boxes of CDs, including the Eric Clapton *Unplugged* my dad gave me in 9th grade to get me into the blues, and the CD the tall man recorded, with a song for me on it, and the U2 *Achtung Baby* that friends chipped in to get for my surprise 16th birthday party. Portishead and Radiohead and Talking Heads, soundtrack to this or that notion. *Physical media,* he said. *It's obsolete.*

That girl from before, she'd have said, *Everything becomes obsolete. That doesn't make it worthless.*

So maybe you can get some things back.

THINGS YOU CAN NEVER REALLY KNOW

How someone might remember you. What you'll come to regret.

How far you have to go to find here.

FIRES

The spark-creak and rise in a fire pit. The sheet-snap in a hearth. Whenever we turn on the gas fireplace in our apartment, the whole room smells like crayons.

We sit on the floor around the coffee table, playing Scrabble for the umpteenth time. I never win. I just stretch out my hand to feel the radiant heat from the fireplace shining on the cat's starboard side.

I watch him, in his mustard-yellow hoodie, sliver wood for kindling. I'm sitting at a picnic table, taking an avocado apart, listening to the dog in the river a few paces away. Now he's blowing gently into the stone drum where the fire will hatch. He stands, claps his hands and rubs them together. *All right,* he says. *Let's burn some steaks.*

Some fires are very small, like fire atop a candle. The little cat walked her tail through it once, and licked the coarse fur for the rest of the day.

Or like the fire on the oven's floor, when the pepper I was roasting burst too early and a bit of its flesh seared to the filament.

Some fires, like the bonfire we built out at the Sun Tunnels, are bigger, and that one kept popping green and neon blue from the paint or veneer or whatever was all over the salvaged four-by-fours. We stood as close as we could without setting ourselves ablaze, kept throwing on fuel to keep the fanged and hungry cold at bay.

But some fires fill the valley with the smell of burning. A little ash drifts down around your shade umbrella into your pasta salad.

I'm sitting in the cafe, missing the man in the mustard-yellow hoodie, when in saunters a group of handsome, filthy men in knee-high work boots and identical T-shirts: Lone Peak Hot Shots. The valley air has been thickening for days while two serpentine fires hatched from lightning-struck embers breathe their way down canyon, and canyon. These are the wild-haired youths whose job it is to lash them into submission, now collecting their iced lattes and bagels.

To be redeemed from fire by fire.

Years ago, one such fellow told me that so much fire moving the way it does—it undulates, the fire and its seven veils—can mesmerize a man, so by the time he realizes how close it is, fire has its lethal tongue in his ear.

Not long after, Margaret and I will be going to sleep in a steep Andean valley, while up the black peaks, a terrible crest of flames shakes itself fuller and fuller in the black. It makes a dangerous orange fortification around the small village, its roof-tiles watched over by so many little guardian bulls, cobbled streets guttered with running water. The same smell of woodsmoke, but different. Like something ancient, without challenger. Like something mean I feared had hatched in me. All night long, I could hear it crumpling and uncrumpling itself in the dark.

When the tongues of flames are in-folded
Into the crowned knot of fire
And the fire and the rose are one.

Sometimes, driving down the West, you'll come to a place along the road where everything is blackened, soft, and you can still see tattered remnants of flame. They do this periodically to clear out the duff, to keep conditions from becoming catastrophic, to make room for some new not-yet-thought-of thing.

ACKNOWLEDGMENTS

Many thanks to the Dorothy Sargent Rosenberg Poetry Prizes, The MacDowell Colony, the National Endowment for the Arts, and the Amy Lowell Poetry Travelling Scholarship, which generously supported the completion of this project.

Many thanks to the *Believer, Third Coast, Anti, Witness,* and *Pear Noir,* for publishing (sometimes in early versions) several of these poems, and to *Western Humanities Review* and *Barrow Street,* for publishing early efforts at this project.

An enduring debt of gratitude to Stephanie G'Schwind and Donald Revell, and all at Colorado State University's Center for Literary Publishing and the Mountain West Poetry Series, for making this a book.

Thanks beyond measure to Claudia Keelan, Derek Henderson, Sara Eliza Johnson, Margaret Reges, Jess Piazza, Taylor Baldwin, Joseph Massey, Joseph Barnes, Laurel Richardson, and others who helped keep me—and this—from careening too much off the rails.

Thanks to Joseph Bradbury, who helped me to refine many of these ideas.

Thank to Dr. Albert Vitale, my friend and keeper, and to Donna Wahoff-Stice. Because of them, I can see to write, and see what I want to write about.

Deep thanks to Hoschi Lewerenz for breathing joy back into this project, and so many of the days spent working on it.

And as ever, thank you to my family, who are enduringly, relentlessly there for me, and who continue to egg me on in foolhardy pursuits like this one.

This book is set in Centaur MT
by the Center for Literary Publishing
at Colorado State University.
Copyediting by Abigail Kerstetter.
Proofreading by Drew Webster.
Book design and typesetting
by Kristin George Bagdanov.
Cover design by Kaelyn Riley.
Printing by BookMobile.